LISTS TO LIVE BY

— *for* —

SMART LIVING

COMPILED BY ALICE GRAY,
STEVE STEPHENS, JOHN VAN DIEST

Multnomah® Publishers *Sisters, Oregon*

LISTS TO LIVE BY FOR SMART LIVING
published by Multnomah Publishers, Inc.
© 2002 by Alice Gray, Steve Stephens, John Van Diest
International Standard Book Number: 1-59052-057-2

Cover image by David Uttley/UDG DesignWorks
Cover image by Photodisc

Scripture quotations are from:
The Holy Bible, New International Version
© 1973, 1984 by International Bible Society,
used by permission of Zondervan Publishing House

Multnomah is a trademark of Multnomah Publishers, Inc.,
and is registered in the U.S. Patent and Trademark Office.
The colophon is a trademark of Multnomah Publishers, Inc.

Printed in the United States of America

For information:
MULTNOMAH PUBLISHERS, INC.
POST OFFICE BOX 1720
SISTERS, OREGON 97759

Lists to live by for smart living / compiled by Alice Gray, Steve Stephens, John Van Diest.
    p. cm.
  ISBN 1-59052-057-2 (pbk.)
    1. Conduct of life--Miscellanea. I. Gray, Alice, 1939- II. Stephens, Steve.
III. Van Diest, John.

BJ1581.2.L56 2002
646.7--dc21

                                                                2002005976

02 03 04 05 06 07 08—10 9 8 7 6 5 4 3 2 1 0

LISTS TO LIVE BY

—— *for* ——

SMART LIVING

Books in the Lists to Live By series:

Lists to Live By: The First Collection

Lists to Live By: The Second Collection

Lists to Live By: The Third Collection

Lists to Live By: The Fourth Collection (December 2002)

Lists to Live By for Every Married Couple

Lists to Live By for Every Caring Family

Lists to Live By for Simple Living

Lists to Live By for Smart Living

Contents

Introduction

Someone once said:

Half of what is written is not read,
Half of what is read is not understood,
Half of what is understood is not believed, and
The remaining half is so insignificant that it doesn't
matter anyway!

If this is true, relax. We've done the work for you. We've sifted through all the information that is not read, not understood, not believed, and not significant. What remain are essential, powerful, and easy-to-read lists for people who want to live smart. These are the treasured gems for everything that really matters.

—ALICE GRAY, DR. STEVE STEPHENS, AND JOHN VAN DIEST

Seven Favorite Quotations of Zig Ziglar

1. Happiness is not a when or a where, but a here and a now!

2. When you associate with winners, your chances of winning go up!

3. You don't have to be great to start, but you have to start to be great.

4. If you aren't on fire, then your wood is wet.

5. I'm not going to ease up, slow up, or give up until I'm taken up.

6. You don't drown by falling into water. You only drown if you stay there.

7. You can have everything in life you want if you will just help enough other people get what they want.

ZIG ZIGLAR
Author of *See You at the Top*

Five Reasons It's Easier to Succeed

1. It's easier to succeed because failure exacts a high price in terms of time when you have to do a job over.

2. It's easier to succeed because success eliminates the agony and frustration of defeat.

3. It's easier to succeed because money spent to fail must be spent again to succeed.

4. It's easier to succeed because a person's credibility decreases with each failure, making it harder to succeed the second time.

5. And it's easier to succeed because joy and expressions of affirmation come from succeeding, whereas feelings of discouragement and discontent accompany failure.

S. TRUETT CATHY, FOUNDER, CHICK-FIL-A COMPANY
From *It's Easier to Succeed Than to Fail*

Your Future Depends On...

Who you will be in the next five years depends on three things:

⁜ the books you read

⁜ the people you meet

⁜ the choices you make

BOB AND EMILIE BARNES
From *The 15 Minute Money Manager*

Destiny

Watch your thoughts; they become words.

Watch your words; they become actions.

Watch your actions; they become habits.

Watch your habits; they become character.

Watch your character; it becomes your destiny.

FRANK OUTLAW
As cited in *More of the Best of Bits & Pieces,* Rob Gilbert, Ph.D., ed.

Things You Need to Know about Failure

1. *To fail is not the same as being a failure.*

   One may have many failings and yet still be far from being a failure.

2. *To fail is not the disgrace everyone thinks it is.*

   To err is to do nothing more than to join the human race.

3. *Failure is only a temporary setback.*

   Failure is never the final chapter of the book of your life unless you give up and quit.

4. *Nothing worthwhile is ever achieved without running the risk of failure.*

   The man who risks everything to try to achieve something truly worthwhile and fails is anything but a disgraceful failure.

5. *Failure is a natural preparation for success.*

   Strange as it may seem to some of you, success is much more difficult to live with successfully than is failure.

6. *Every failing brings with it the possibility of something greater.*

   Analyze failure under whatever circumstances you choose, and you will discover some seeds for turning failure into success.

7. *What you do with failures in your life is up to you.*

   Failure is either a blessing or a curse, depending upon the
   individual's reaction or response to it.

8. *Failings are opportunities to learn how to do things better the*
   next time—to learn where the pitfalls are and how to avoid them.
   The best possible thing to do with failure is to learn all you
   can from it.

DALE GALLOWAY
Dean, Asbury Theological Seminary
From *How to Feel Like a Somebody Again!*

Wisdom *for* Smart Living

*The door of wisdom swings on hinges
of common sense and uncommon thoughts.*

—WILLIAM A. WARD

*Wisdom is knowing what to do next;
virtue is doing it.*

—DAVID STARR JORDAN

*Ignorance or arrogance
can place one in harm's way.*

—AUTHOR UNKNOWN

*Eyes that look are common.
Eyes that see are rare.*

—J. OSWALD SANDERS

Eight Significant Choices

1. To resist pain or use it

2. To gather wealth or gather grace

3. To speak wisely or foolishly

4. To value your time or fritter it away

5. To live for self or for what is right

6. To develop your talents or waste them

7. To persevere or protest

8. To stand for truth or abandon it

JILL BRISCOE
Adapted from *8 Choices That Can Change a Woman's Life*

Five Steps to Better Behavior

✣ Be consistent.

✣ Stay cool.

✣ Clarify the consequences.

✣ Be forgiving.

✣ Overlook past offenses.

GARY D. CHAPMAN
Condensed from *Christian Parenting Today* magazine

How to Keep Your Resolutions

1. Write them down.

2. Count the cost.

3. Make them meaningful.

4. Give them priority.

5. Be specific and practical.

6. Ask someone to keep you accountable.

7. Seek help if you struggle.

8. Break them into steps.

9. Reward yourself for each successful step.

10. Keep your eyes on the goal.

11. Do all you can to make them fun.

12. Pray.

JOHN VAN DIEST
Associate publisher

Gift of Success

THE GIFT OF DISCERNMENT:

*I will distinguish the difference
between truth and error, right and wrong,
good and evil.*

A Short Course in Human Relations

The six most important words: "I admit I made a mistake."

The five most important words: "You did a good job."

The four most important words: "What is your opinion?"

The three most important words: "If you please."

The two most important words: "Thank you."

The one most important word: "We."

The least important word: "I."

AUTHOR UNKNOWN

As cited in *More of the Best of Bits & Pieces,* Rob Gilbert, Ph.D., editor

Actions That Take Courage

- Admitting you are wrong.

- Doing what is right when everyone else isn't.

- Speaking to someone you don't know.

- Saying "no" when people are trying to get you to do something you know you shouldn't.

- Telling the truth and accepting the consequences.

- Standing up for something you believe in even though it might mean rejection or ridicule or even physical harm.

- Defending someone who is considered unpopular or unacceptable.

- Facing a limitation and giving it your very best regardless of pain or discomforts.

- Confronting a fear without running away.

- Giving sacrificially to protect or promote someone you love, someone who has been wronged, or someone who is in need.

- Taking a risk.

- Sharing your heart honestly including your feelings and fears and failures.

- Living your faith with all your heart, mind, soul, and strength regardless of the cost.

- Being the only one.

DR. STEVE STEPHENS
Psychologist and seminar speaker

11 Things to Remember

The value of time

The success of perseverance

The pleasure of working

The dignity of simplicity

The worth of character

The power of kindness

The influence of example

The obligation of duty

The wisdom of economy

The improvement of talent

The joy of originating

MARSHALL FIELD
Department store magnate

Ten Life-Defining Moments

1. When called to obey

2. When seeking to be known

3. When faced with failure

4. When pursuing your purpose

5. When taking a stand

6. When engaged in suffering

7. When asked to forgive

8. When experiencing temptation

9. When needing to repent

10. When deciding on God

JAMES EMERY WHITE
Condensed from *Life-Defining Moments*

People with Character

They walk with integrity.

They do what is right.

They tell the truth.

They don't gossip.

They don't mistreat people.

They side with those who are right.

They keep their word.

They lend interest-free money to those in need.

They don't take advantage of people for financial gain.

ADAPTED FROM THE PSALMS

From *A Diamond in the Rough,* compiled by Andrew Stanley

Gift of Success

THE GIFT OF INTEGRITY:

I will follow the path that is
true, right, good, and wise,
regardless of where it might lead.

What Is Success?

* To laugh often and love much;

* To win the respect of intelligent people and the affection of children;

* To earn the approval of honest critics and endure the betrayal of false friends;

* To appreciate beauty;

* To find the best in others;

* To give of oneself;

- To leave the world a bit better, whether by a healthy child, a garden patch, or a redeemed social condition;

- To play and laugh with enthusiasm and sing with exultation;

- To know even one life has breathed easier because you have lived…

- This is to have succeeded.

RALPH WALDO EMERSON
Poet, essayist, and philosopher

Take Nothing for Granted

For every right that you cherish,

    you have a duty which you must fulfill.

For every hope that you entertain,

    you have a task that you must perform.

For every good that you wish to preserve,

    you will have to sacrifice your comfort and your ease.

There is nothing for nothing any longer.

GEORGE WASHINGTON
First president of the United States

Traits of a Wise Person

- Consciousness of an honest purpose of life.

- A just estimate of oneself and everyone else.

- Frequent self-examinations.

- Steady obedience to what one knows to be right.

- Indifference to what others may think or say.

MARCUS AURELIUS
Roman emperor

12 Lessons Worth Repeating

1. Be honest.

2. Set goals and work quietly and systematically toward them.

3. Assign a task to yourself.

4. Never give up.

5. Be confident that you can make a difference.

6. Don't ever stop learning and improving.

7. Slow down and live.

8. Choose your friends carefully.

9. Be a can-do and will-try person.

10. Try to live in the present.

11. You are in charge of your own attitude.

12. Always remember that you are never alone.

MARIAN WRIGHT EDELMAN
Condensed from *The Measure of Our Success*

Wisdom *for* Smart Living

In matters of principle, stand like a rock;

in matters of taste, swim with the current.

—THOMAS JEFFERSON

If any of you lacks wisdom, he should ask God,

who gives generously to all without finding fault,

and it will be given to him.

—ST. JAMES

Here I stand on the edge of an ocean of truth.

I have picked up a few grains of sand,

but the whole ocean lies before me unknown.

—SIR ISAAC NEWTON

Every Night We Should Ask Ourselves...

What infirmity have I mastered today?

What passions have I opposed?

What temptation have I resisted?

What virtue have I acquired?

SENECA

Philosopher and playwright

The Better Way

Excellence is willing to be wrong,
Perfection is being right.

Excellence is risk,
Perfection is fear.

Excellence is powerful,
Perfection is anger and frustration.

Excellence is spontaneous,
Perfection is control.

Excellence is acceptance,
Perfection is judgment.

Excellence is giving,
Perfection is taking.

Excellence is confidence,
Perfection is doubt.

Excellence is flowing,
Perfection is pressure.

Excellence is journey,
Perfection is destination.

AUTHOR UNKNOWN
From *Finding a Mentor, Being a Mentor*

13 Rules to Live By

- It ain't as bad as you think; it will look better in the morning.

- Get mad, then get over it.

- Avoid having your ego so close to your position that when your position falls, your ego goes with it.

- It can be done!

- Be careful what you choose. You may get it.

- Don't let adverse facts stand in the way of a good decision.

- Check small things.

- Share credit.

- You can't make someone else's choices. You shouldn't let someone else make yours.

- Remain calm. Be kind.

- Have a vision. Be demanding.

- Don't take counsel of your fears or naysayers.

- Perpetual optimism is a force multiplier. (In the military, one is always looking for methods of increasing or multiplying one's forces.)

GENERAL (RET) COLIN L. POWELL

People Who Make a Difference Have...

INITIATIVE—being a self-starter with contagious energy.

VISION—seeing beyond the obvious, claiming new objectives.

UNSELFISHNESS—releasing the controls and the glory.

TEAMWORK—involving, encouraging, and supporting others.

FAITHFULNESS—hanging in there, in season and out.

ENTHUSIASM—providing affirmation and excitement to the task.

DISCIPLINE—modeling great character regardless of the odds.

CONFIDENCE—representing security, faith, and determination.

CHARLES R. SWINDOLL
From *The Tale of the Tardy Oxcart*

Six Destructive Mistakes

1. The delusion that personal gain is made by crushing others.

2. The tendency to worry about things that cannot be changed or corrected.

3. Insisting that a thing is impossible because we cannot accomplish it.

4. Refusing to set aside trivial preferences.

5. Neglecting development and refinement of the mind, and not acquiring the habit of reading and studying.

6. Attempting to compel others to believe and live as we do.

MARCUS TULLIUS CICERO
Statesman, philosopher, and orator

Thoughts that Hold Us Back

I can't

That's a problem

That's not fair

I won't

Stupid

Never

It won't work

It's been tried before

It's too hard

Impossible

It's hopeless

I'm not good enough

I'll get even

JOHN VAN DIEST
Associate publisher

Gift of Success

THE GIFT OF DISCOVERY:

*I will ask for wisdom
and perspective from others while
seeking guidance from God.*

20 Power Thoughts

1. Curiosity leads to creativity.

2. Trust your positive instincts.

3. When it's dark, look for the stars.

4. Faith is always stronger than failure.

5. Build a dream and the dream builds you.

6. Obstacles are opportunities in disguise.

7. When the going gets tough—laugh.

8. Don't miss the best things in life.

9. Itemize your assets.

10. Fix the problem, not the blame.

11. Share the credit.

12. Never make an irreversible decision in a down time.

13. Treasure time like gold.

14. Never judge reality by your limited experiences.

15. You will never win if you never begin.

16. Success without conflict is unrealistic.

17. Make sure your dreams are big enough for God to fit in.

18. Never let a problem become an excuse.

19. When it looks like you've exhausted all possibilities, remember this: You haven't.

20. Always look at what you have left. Never look at what you have lost.

ROBERT H. SCHULLER
From *Power Thoughts*

Three Great Essentials

Three essentials for achieving anything worthwhile:

⊹ Hard work

⊹ Stick-to-itiveness

⊹ Common sense

THOMAS EDISON
Inventor

Gift of Success

THE GIFT OF PERSISTENCE:

I will tenaciously pursue
an admirable goal even when
there are obstacles.

Criticism Kills...

* Motivation

* Enthusiasm

* Confidence

* Joy

* Dreams

* Hope

* Spirit

DR. STEVE STEPHENS
Psychologist and seminar speaker

Contrasts for Life

Bitterness imprisons life; love releases it.

Bitterness paralyzes life; love empowers it.

Bitterness sickens life; love heals it.

Bitterness blinds life; love anoints its eyes.

HARRY EMERSON FOSDICK
From *Riverside Sermons*

Three Things That Cultivate Genius

1. Contentment of mind

2. Cherishing good thoughts

3. Exercising the memory

ROBERT SOUTHEY
English author

Gift of Success

THE GIFT OF SENSITIVITY:

*I will find the balance
between love and truth so that neither
virtue is diminished.*

Golden Threads of a Successful Life

- People who know the most know that they know so little, while people who know nothing want to take all day to tell you about it.

- Self-improvement can be harmful if you are doing it to look better. If you live your life helping others look better, you'll become better without trying.

- If you give in order to get something, you're not really giving—you're trading.

- Big people are always giving someone credit and taking blame; little people are always seeking credit and placing blame.

- Don't worry about having to make a right decision. Make your decision and then work to make it right.

- An attitude of gratitude should flavor everything you do. Learning to be thankful is the golden thread woven through every truly successful life.

CHARLIE "TREMENDOUS" JONES
President, Life Management Services, Inc.
Condensed from *Life Is Tremendous*

*The art of being wise is the
art of knowing what to overlook.*

—WILLIAM JAMES

*Consult not your fears, but your hopes and dreams.
Think not about your frustrations,
but about your unfulfilled potential.
Concern yourself not with your failures,
but with all that is still possible for you to do.*

—POPE JOHN XXIII

*I have often regretted my speech,
never my silence.*

—PUBLILIUS SYRUS

Wanted!

More to *improve*

and fewer to *disapprove*.

More *doers*

and fewer *talkers*.

More to say *It can be done*

and fewer to say *It's impossible*.

More to *inspire* others

and fewer to *throw cold water* on them.

More to get *into the thick of things*

and fewer to *sit on the sidelines*.

More to point out *what's right*

and fewer to show *what's wrong*.

More to *light a candle*

and fewer to *curse the darkness*.

AUTHOR UNKNOWN

How to Handle Criticism

1. Listen.

Don't begin thinking of your "defense" while they are still talking. Take a deep breath and try to stay calm until they are finished.

2. Avoid retaliation.

No matter how harsh or unjustified a person may come across, control your emotions. If you get angry it will only escalate the situation and cause further turmoil. The Bible says *a gentle answer turns away wrath.*

3. Don't respond immediately.

Say you will consider what has been said and that you will get back to them in a day or two. And then do it!

4. Respect the criticism.

Even if the criticism seems unfair, there may be some truth to it. Look at criticism as an *opportunity* to become a better person, worker, friend, or family member.

5. *Be honest with yourself.*

Consider what was said, focus on the truth, and make a plan to change what you can.

6. *Forgive.*

If they were abrasive in their approach, forgive them, and don't hold it against them in the future.

7. *Have a good attitude.*

Even if you think the criticism was undeserved or severe, thank the person for communicating their concerns to you. Remember that every situation in life will make you bitter or better—it's your choice.

KYLE LIEDTKE
Media consultant

Seven Essentials

1. Don't waste.

2. Work hard.

3. Don't cut corners.

4. Have fun doing things.

5. Be strict but caring.

6. Tackle problems head-on.

7. Pray.

GRANDMA SINCLAIR
Grandmother of Dave Thomas, founder of Wendy's
From *Dave Says...Well Done!*

Gift of Success

THE GIFT OF EXAMPLE:

*I will intentionally provide a
role model that will influence others
by positive example.*

Be

Be understanding to your enemies.

Be loyal to your friends.

Be strong enough to face the world each day.

Be weak enough to know you cannot do everything alone.

Be generous to those who need your help.

Be frugal with what you need yourself.

Be wise enough to know that you do not know everything.

Be foolish enough to believe in miracles.

Be willing to share your joys.

Be willing to share the sorrows of others.

Be a leader when you see a path others have missed.

Be a follower when you are shrouded by the mists of uncertainty.

Be the first to congratulate an opponent who succeeds.

Be the last to criticize a colleague who fails.

Be sure where your next step will fall, so that you will not stumble.

Be sure of your final destination, in case you are going the wrong way.

Be loving to those who do not love you, and they may change.

Above all, be yourself.

AUTHOR UNKNOWN

How to Become a Lifelong Learner

1. Start with your attitude.

Lifelong learning begins with a heart that desires change, wisdom, and application.

2. Ask questions.

Learners ask good questions. They possess an insatiable curiosity—a longing to know, discover, inquire. Ask questions that get below the surface.

3. Join others.

Collaborative learning—in classes, small groups, with friends and colleagues—allows us to benefit from diverse perspectives and approaches. People are a gold mine of learning that is tapped through conversation.

4. Check out the other side.

Take time to examine and understand another point of view, even if it radically contradicts yours. You may see things in a new light, or you may have your old convictions strengthened. Personal convictions that have never been tested remain flabby.

5. Read broadly.

Include a diversity of books, authors, and topics. Resist the temptation to read only those books that reinforce what you already believe.

6. Keep a journal.

Recording what you learn captures your growth in wisdom.

7. *Experiment.*

Try new approaches and ideas. Age does not affect your ability to learn. An eighty-year-old can learn to surf the Net like an eighteen-year-old.

8. *Apply what you know.*

Our depth of understanding is often directly related to our ability to apply what we've learned. Application takes knowledge from the head to the heart.

BILL MOWRY
From *Discipleship Journal*

Gift of Success

THE GIFT OF NOBILITY:

I will keep my word and my commitments regardless of more tempting opportunities.

How to Remember What You Read

HIGHLIGHT

Always keep a highlighter with you
and mark meaningful quotes or impacting principles.

WRITE

Record the most important ideas in your journal and review
them from time to time.

ASK

Read actively by asking yourself questions, like:

> *What is the author's purpose in writing this book?*
> *What's the key idea of the book?*
> *How can this book help me in my life?*

THINK

Ponder what you read. As one old sage said, "It is better to master 10 books than just read 1,000."

SPEAK

Share with a friend some of the principles you've learned and how they have affected your life.

KYLE LIEDTKE
Media consultant

Four Ways to Grow Old Gracefully

1. Fear less; hope more.

2. Eat less; chew more.

3. Talk less; say more.

4. Hate less; love more.

FROM A "DEAR ABBY" NEWSPAPER COLUMN

Five Tips for Staying Young

1. Your mind is not old; keep developing it.

2. Your humor is not over; keep enjoying it.

3. Your strength is not gone; keep using it.

4. Your opportunities have not vanished; keep pursuing them.

5. God is not dead; keep seeking Him.

AUTHOR UNKNOWN

Ten Secrets to Ageless Living

1. Never let age get in the way of life.

2. Stay curious, explore, discover, and continue to learn new things.

3. Play, have fun, be happy, and maintain a zest for life by being vital.

4. Keep the brain and the body busy; stimulate the mind, eat healthily, exercise.

5. Smile, laugh, maintain a sense of humor, and always stay young at heart.

6. Have a positive attitude and outlook, and be optimistic to overcome challenges.

7. Believe in yourself by having faith, hope, spirit, value, meaning, and purpose.

8. Stay connected, engaged, creative, and useful by continuing to contribute.

9. Find fulfillment, peace, serenity, and self-esteem by giving back—volunteer.

10. Enjoy and cherish healthy relationships with loved ones, friends, and family.

KELLY FERRIN
From *What's Age Got to Do with It?*

Wisdom *for* Smart Living

Blessed is the one who finds wisdom…
for she is more precious than silver and yields better
than gold… Long life is in her right hand;
riches and honor are in her left.
Her ways are pleasant, and all her paths are peace.

—SOLOMON

From listening comes wisdom,
from speaking comes repentance.

—ITALIAN PROVERB

The price for anything worth having
is work, patience, love, and self-sacrifice.

—JOHN BURROUGHS

Life 101

I'm learning...

- that a good sense of humor is money in the bank. In life. On the job. In a marriage.

- that a good attitude can control situations you can't. That any bad experience can be a good one. It all depends on me.

- to slow down more often and enjoy the trip. To eat more ice cream and less bran.

- that you can do something in an instant that will give you heartache for life.

- that bitterness and gossip accomplish nothing, but forgiveness and love accomplish everything.

- that it takes years to build trust and seconds to destroy it.

- that if I'm standing on the edge of a cliff, the best way forward is to back up.

- that you don't fail when you lose; you fail when you quit.

- that too many people spend a lifetime stealing time from those who love them the most, trying to please the ones who care about them the least.

- that money is a lousy way of keeping score. That true success isn't measured in cars or homes or bank accounts, but in relationships.

- that having enough money isn't nearly as much fun as I thought it would be when I didn't have any. That money buys less than you think.

- that helping another is far more rewarding than helping myself. That those who laugh more worry less.

- that you cannot make anyone love you. But you can work on being lovable.

- that degrees, credentials, and awards mean far less than I thought they would.

- that I will never regret a moment spent reading the Bible or praying. Or a kind word. Or a day at the beach.

- that laughter and tears are nothing to be ashamed of. To celebrate the good things. And pray about the bad.

- And I'm learning that the most important thing in the world is loving God. That everything good comes from that.

PHIL CALLAWAY
Condensed from *Who Put the Skunk in the Trunk?*

Vital Questions

Ask yourself:

What are the options?

What are my priorities?

How can I grow?

Ask others:

Will you forgive me?

Will you help me?

What can I do for you?

Ask God:

Who am I?

What is Your will?

What is eternal?

DAVID SANFORD
Coauthor, *God Is Relevant*

Gift of Success

THE GIFT OF DEFERENCE:

I will cheerfully submit to those in authority unless obedience compromises God's commandments.

When Not to Speak

1. When you're in the heat of anger.

2. When you don't have all the facts.

3. When it is time to listen.

4. When you are tempted to joke about something serious.

5. When you would be ashamed of your words later.

6. When your words might convey the wrong impression.

7. When the issue is none of your business.

8. When you are tempted to tell an outright lie.

9. When your words will damage someone else's reputation.

10. When your words might hurt a friendship.

11. When you may have to eat your words later.

12. When you have already said too much.

13. When you have promised to keep a confidence.

14. When you tend to talk before thinking.

15. When your words stir up dissension.

16. When you are tempted to praise yourself.

ADAPTED FROM THE BOOK OF PROVERBS

Wisdom for Smart Living

*My faith demands that I do
whatever I can, whenever I can,
for as long as I can, with whatever I have
to try to make a difference.*

—JIMMY CARTER

*Coming together is a beginning;
keeping together is progress;
working together is success.*

—HENRY FORD

*The most important thing in communication
is to hear what isn't being said.*

—PETER DRUCKER

Wisdom is the right use of knowledge.

—CHARLES SPURGEON

We Are Shaped By...

Friends.

Literature.

Music.

Pleasures.

Ambitions.

Thoughts.

A. W. TOZER
From *The Quotable Tozer*

12 Steps to Creative Thinking

1. *Right away, write it down.*

   Record ideas as soon as you think of them. Keep paper and pen handy at all times—in your car, by your television, on your nightstand.

2. *Listen to music.*

   Listen to whatever sparks your imagination, whether it's Bach, the Beatles, or something you've never heard before.

3. *Exercise.*

   Go for a run, shoot some hoops, do jumping jacks—anything that starts your blood pumping and keeps your mind sharp.

4. *Brainstorm with a friend, coworker, or six-year-old.*

   Talk with someone who looks at the world a little differently than you do. Chances are he or she will inspire a new approach.

5. *Do it poorly.*

   If you're a perfectionist, don't be. Create something that isn't necessarily your best work, but that gets the job done. Then go back later to fix it or redo it.

6. *Watch people.*

   Go downtown or to the mall, sit on a bench, and observe the passersby. Imagine what kind of life they lead.

7. *Keep a journal.*

   Write about your life and what's important to you, then revisit your old thoughts when you need new ideas.

8. *Pray or read the Bible.*

   Putting life into spiritual perspective can take the pressure off and jump-start the creative juices.

9. *Free-write.*

Sit down at the computer or with pen and paper and write whatever comes into your mind. Watch what comes out!

10. *Change your locale.*

Find a new quiet place—a park, the beach, a library, or just a different room—and let your mind wander.

11. *Wash the dishes or mow the lawn.*

It's easy and it gives you a feeling of accomplishment while you're trying to think.

12. *Sleep on it.*

If nothing is working, your best bet may be to give up for now. Let your subconscious create overnight, and you'll have fresh ideas tomorrow.

JAMES LUND
Writer

The Credit Belongs to the Man Who...

* strives valiantly.

* knows great enthusiasm and great devotion.

* spends himself in a worthy cause.

* at the best knows the triumph of high achievement.

* at the worst fails while daring greatly.

THEODORE ROOSEVELT
Twenty-sixth president of the United States

Three Pillars of Learning

1. Seeing much.

2. Suffering much.

3. Studying much.

SIR BENJAMIN DISRAELI
Former British prime minister

All that is beautiful God has made.

He sets eternity in our hearts.

No one can fathom the work of God—

where it will end, or where it starts.

—SOLOMON

Our thinking guides our choices;

choices become habits,

habits create character.

—CHUCK COLSON

He is no fool who gives what

he cannot keep to gain that which

he cannot lose.

—JIM ELLIOT

Goals for Authentic Growth

I will have a passion for excellence.

I will ask, listen, and hear—to determine the wants, needs, and possibilities of all with whom I come in contact.

I will provide an example of commitment and integrity.

I will follow a path of continual empowerment for myself and others.

I will constantly focus on the strengths of all with whom I come in contact.

I will cultivate optimum physical, mental, and spiritual fitness.

I will lead as I would like to be led.

I will savor the flavor of each passing moment.

I will infuse every thought and relationship with faith, hope, love, and gratitude.

JOE D. BATTEN
From *New Man* magazine

Wise Sayings

1. Never put off till tomorrow what you can do today.

2. Never trouble another for what you can do yourself.

3. Never spend your money before you have it.

4. Never buy what you do not want because it is cheap.

5. Pride costs us more than hunger, thirst, and cold.

6. We never repent of having eaten too little.

7. Nothing is troublesome that we do willingly.

8. How much pain the evils, which have never happened, have cost us.

9. Take things always by their smooth handle.

10. When angry, count to ten before you speak; if very angry, a hundred.

THOMAS JEFFERSON
Third president of the United States

Why We Procrastinate

We feel overwhelmed.

We overestimate the amount of time needed.

We would rather be doing something else.

We think that if we wait long enough, the task will go away.

We fear failure.

We fear success.

We enjoy the last-minute adrenaline rush.

BOB AND EMILIE BARNES
From *The 15 Minute Money Manager*

Gift of Success

THE GIFT OF FAIRNESS:

I will resolve conflicts in a way that is just without yielding to threat, prejudice, or personal preference.

Great Ways to Help Others Reach Their Goals

Applaud the tiniest of successes.

Share your own experiences.

Talk often about their goals.

Support them during difficult times.

Send letters and notes of encouragement.

Buy little gifts as rewards.

Keep track of their record.

CYNDI HAYNES
From *The Book of Change*

Smart Goals Are....

✢ Specific

✢ Measurable

✢ Achievable

✢ Realistic

✢ Timed

ALICE GRAY
Inspirational conference speaker

Gift of Success

THE GIFT OF PRIORITIES:

I will choose to treasure relationships rather than things that have no true lasting value.

Better Your Life

1. Avoid gossip.

2. Release bitterness.

3. Take risks.

4. Trust.

5. Don't live for "stuff."

6. Master your appetites.

7. Grow deep.

8. Be generous.

9. Think globally.

PAUL BORTHWICK
Senior consultant, Development Associates International
From *Discipleship Journal*

Five Ways to Start the New Year Right

1. Don't make resolutions.

Make plans. Resolutions are pie-in-the-sky, down-the-road goals. Plans are doable, step-by-step.

2. Turn the TV off.

Think how much time you could have to accomplish dreams if you used even the daily half hour you normally watch TV.

3. Learn to say no.

Prioritize instead of becoming overwhelmed with all your to-dos and opportunities. Include time for rest and recreation and time for meditation.

4. *Write thank-you notes for simple reasons.*

Gratitude is a priceless gift, so give it freely!

5. *Pray about everything.*

Talk to God about everyday details as well as big-picture items.

Nothing is too small—or too big—for Him to care about.

LIITA FORSYTH
From *Virtue* magazine

Proper Money Management

1. Give some away.

2. Keep some.

3. It is better not to borrow; but if you cannot avoid it, repay the debt quickly.

4. Do not spend money that doesn't belong to you.

5. Do not become preoccupied with money.

6. Don't fall in love with money!

MARY HUNT

From *The Financially Confident Woman*

Wisdom *for* Smart Living

Pain makes man think.
Thought makes man wise.
Wisdom makes life endurable.
—JOHN PATRICK

It is well for one to know more than he says.
—TITUS MACCIUS PLAUTUS

Don't hurt yourself, and don't hurt others.
Take care of yourself so you can take care of others.
—PETER MCWILLIAMS

Financial Perspective

1. Realize that money can't make you happy.

2. Live for what really matters.

3. Know that riches will pass away.

4. Be content with what you have.

5. Put people above money.

6. Share what you have with the ones you love.

7. Invest in the right places.

8. Keep character above acquiring.

9. Don't cling to what you have.

10. Give generously to things that will last beyond your lifetime.

JOHN VAN DIEST
Associate publisher

How to Break a Bad Habit

Is it harmful to others or me?

> You must be convinced it's bad.

What are the consequences of not stopping?

> Calculate the real cost in time, money, and health.

Does it grieve God, family, or friends?

> Decide if you are willing to risk these relationships.

Do you really want to change?

> You will need both desire and perseverance.

Can you admit your need for help?

> If your answer is yes, you must take the next step.

Will you seek support from others?

> There is an array of help available for those who ask.

DR. JOSEPH C. ALDRICH
President emeritus, Multnomah Bible College and Seminary

Wisdom of Abraham Lincoln

- You are only what you are when no one is looking.

- Character is like a tree, and reputation is like a shadow. The shadow is what we think of it; the tree is the real thing.

- I have simply tried to do what seemed best each day, as each day came.

- To sit by in silence, when they should protest, makes cowards of men.

- It often requires more courage to dare to do right, than to fear to do wrong.

- Those who deny freedom to others deserve it not for themselves. And, under a just God, cannot long retain it.

- The better part of one's life consists of his friendships.

- It is more important to know that we are on God's side.

- A good laugh is good for both the mental and physical digestion.

- You cannot help men permanently by doing for them what they could and should do for themselves.

- Nearly all men can stand adversity, but if you want to test a man's character, give him power.

- Let minor differences and personal preferences, if there be such, go to the winds.

Abraham Lincoln
Sixteenth president of the United States

Gift of Success

THE GIFT OF HONOR:

*I will notice and applaud the
success of others and encourage them
toward their personal best.*

Vision

✤ A vision without a task is but a dream.

✤ A task without vision is drudgery.

✤ A vision with a task is the hope of the world.

ON THE CORNERSTONE OF A CHURCH IN ENGLAND
DATED 1730

The Way to Fulfillment

Think rightly.

Feel deeply.

Choose wisely.

Act accordingly.

Live intentionally.

LOREN FISCHER
Professor and pastor

Don'ts for Decision Making

- Don't focus on doing more tasks, but on doing fewer tasks well.

- Don't accept impossible deadlines—factor in extra "pad" time.

- Don't leave decisions hanging—decide immediately on a course of action each time you can.

- Don't let the desires of others dictate how you spend your time.

- Don't assume that the "emergencies" of others are your emergencies.

- Don't say yes when you should say no.

JUNE HUNT
From *Healing the Hurting Heart*

Practical Words of a Philosopher

Be gracious.

Know your chief asset and cultivate it.

Never exaggerate.

Do nothing to make you lose respect for yourself.

Have strength of spirit.

Work with good tools.

Keep in mind the happy ending.

To jog the understanding is a greater feat than to jog the memory.

Know how to refuse.

Be alert when seeking information.

Forestall evil gossip.

Be generous in action.

Have a just estimate of yourself.

Attain and maintain a good reputation.

Do not make a show of what you have.

The shortest road to being somebody is to know whom to follow.

Prepare yourself in good fortune, for the bad.

Never cry about your woes.

Know the value of reconsideration.

BALTASAR GRACIÁN
Philosopher

Seven Important Choices

1. Choose a goal.

2. Choose to use wisdom.

3. Choose how you will spend your time.

4. Choose your battles.

5. Choose your words.

6. Choose your friends.

7. Choose your attitude.

SHERI ROSE SHEPHERD
From *7 Ways to Build a Better You*

Seven Important Lessons

1. Learn to respect and esteem others.

2. Learn to maximize your strengths and minimize your weaknesses.

3. Learn to be an encourager.

4. Learn to approach life with joy and hope.

5. Learn to forgive.

6. Learn to treat children special.

7. Learn to seek wisdom.

JOHN VAN DIEST
Associate publisher

Making Today Better

Develop an attitude of gratitude.

Even when you are experiencing tough times, remember the
blessings in your life. It's like sprinkling sunshine on a cloudy day.

Encourage others.

When someone has a goal, most people point out the obstacles.
You be the one to point out the possibilities.

Give sincere compliments.

We all like to be remembered for our best moments.

Keep growing.

Walk a different path. Take a class. Read something inspiring.

Unwrap the gift of forgiveness.

Forgiveness is a blessing for the one who forgives as well as for
the one who is forgiven.

Take care of yourself.

Exercise, eat a healthy diet, and find some quiet moments.

Sing and dance a little bit every day.

A merry heart is good for the soul.

Do random acts of kindness.

The most fun is when the other person doesn't know who did it.

Treasure relationships.

Eat meals together, take walks, listen. Share laughter and tears.
Make memories.

Share your faith.

You can wish someone joy and peace and happy things, but
when you share your faith—you've wished them everything.

ALICE GRAY
Inspirational conference speaker

Lessons from Aesop's Fables

Avoid solutions that are worse than the problem.

It is a great art to do the right thing at the right time.

Example is more powerful than reproach.

Honesty is the best policy.

He who is discontented in one place will seldom be happy in another.

Do boldly what you do at all.

The worth of money is not in its possession, but in its use.

Those who seek to please everybody, please no one.

The memory of a good deed lives on.

Happy is the man who learns from the misfortunes of others.

He who wishes evil for his neighbor brings a curse upon himself.

Do not attempt too much at once.

AESOP
Ancient storyteller

Influential People

We are impacted most by…

1. People of courage

2. People of character

3. People of discipline

4. People of excellence

5. People of compassion

6. People of encouragement

7. People of vision

8. People of generosity

9. People of wisdom

10. People of faith

DR. STEVE STEPHENS
Psychologist and seminar speaker

Gift of Success

THE GIFT OF OPTIMISM:

*I will dwell on what is
positive and focus on the strengths,
talents, and beauty of others.*

Taking Control of Your Time

1. Remember who's in charge. Time is something you manage, not something that manages you. Learn to think through each time commitment in its entirety. Buy yourself time to think by asking, "Can I let you know tomorrow?"

2. Decide what is truly urgent. Rather than think, "I must get this done now!" try putting it off. Surprise! Most "urgent" needs aren't really that urgent.

3. Schedule in reverse. Put the real priorities on the calendar first—family picnic or date night. Then write in everything else.

4. Drop one thing from your schedule. You'll probably let someone down, but look who benefits. Spending two fewer days a month as a lunch monitor at your son's school frees you up for a lunch date with your spouse.

5. *Be, rather than do.* Try it for an evening. Think. Pray. Relax in a lawn chair.

6. *Get your spouse's perspective.* Ask your mate to comment on how you're using your time and what seems to be robbing you of time.

7. *Be honest about your limitations.* Do you find yourself saying yes to a project in the hopes that a weekend will suddenly hold the ten extra hours you'd need to complete it? You can't manufacture time.

8. *Make a list of your commitments.* Post the list next to the phone or your calendar. A visual reminder of all that you're involved with will make you think twice before taking on something else.

LOUISE A. FERREBEE
Associate editor
From *Marriage Partnership* magazine

A life of wisdom…involves simplicity,

independence, magnanimity, and trust.

—HENRY DAVID THOREAU

Knowledge is proud that he has learned so much;

wisdom is humble that he knows no more.

—WILLIAM COWPER

The pessimist complains about the wind;

the optimist expects it to change;

the realist adjusts the sails.

—WILLIAM ARTHUR WARD

Handbook of Wisdom

If you don't have a Bible, get one.

If you've got a Bible, read it.

If you read the Bible, believe it.

If you believe the Bible, live it.

BRUCE & CHERYL BICKEL AND STAN & KARIN JANTZ
From *Life's Little Handbook of Wisdom*

Benjamin Franklin's Ten Virtues

1. Temperance. Eat not to dullness; drink not to elevation.

2. Silence. Speak not but what may benefit others or yourself; avoid trifling conversation.

3. Order. Let all your things have their places; let each part of your business have its time.

4. Resolution. Resolve to perform what you ought; perform without fail what you resolve.

5. Frugality. Make no expense but to do good to others or yourself; waste nothing.

6. Industry. Lose no time; be always employed in something useful; cut off all unnecessary actions.

7. Sincerity. Use no hurtful deceit; think innocently and justly; and if you speak, speak accordingly.

8. Justice. Wrong none by doing injuries or omitting the benefits that are your duty.

9. Moderation. Avoid extremes; forbear resenting injuries so much as you think they deserve.

10. Tranquility. Be not disturbed by trifles or accidents common or unavoidable.

BENJAMIN FRANKLIN

From *The Autobiography and Other Writings by Benjamin Franklin*

Basic Rules from Children

Share.

Don't hit.

Stay on the path.

Don't chew with your mouth open.

Say "Please" and "Thank you."

Don't burp in public.

Be nice to old people.

Close your eyes when you pray.

Put your dishes in the sink.

Don't go through red lights.

Smile.

Hold hands when crossing the street.

Don't pick off scabs.

Brush your teeth.

Clean your room.

Listen.

Don't use bad words.

Don't call names.

Go to church.

Tell jokes.

Obey the rules.

COLLECTED FROM CHILDREN AGES FIVE TO TEN

Kids Say the Smartest Things

- If you want someone to listen to you, whisper it.

- You can't be everyone's best friend.

- All libraries smell the same.

- Sometimes you have to take the test before you've finished studying.

- Silence can be an answer.

- Ask where things come from.

- If you throw a ball at someone, they'll probably throw it back.

- Don't nod on the phone.

- Say grace.

- The best place to be when you are sad is in Grandma's lap.

PHIL CALLAWAY
From *Who Put the Skunk in the Trunk?*

Gift of Success

THE GIFT OF HUMILITY:

I will remember that

without God's blessings and

the help of others, I will not achieve

any measure of success.

A Father's Advice

- Make God and people your top priorities.

- Stop and smell the roses.

- Keep your promises.

- Persevere. Life is tough. Period.

- Express yourself.

- Remember that God molds our character through discomfort, through challenge.

- Choose your friends wisely.

- Let your actions speak louder than your words.

- Remember your roots.

- Laugh, often and loud.

- Learn to discern right from wrong.

- Don't be afraid to say you're sorry.

- Pray.

- Read. Read. Read.

- Humility is a greater virtue than pride.

BOB WELCH
Adapted from *A Father for All Seasons*

Foundation Builders for Your Family

1. Hug and praise them.

2. See discipline as an asset.

3. Create traditions.

4. Cultivate laughter.

5. Stay close to teachers.

6. Be where they are.

7. Share your life with them.

8. Keep a long-range perspective.

SUSAN ALEXANDER YATES
From *How to Like the Ones You Love*

Ladder of Success

Plan purposefully.

Prepare prayerfully.

Proceed positively.

Pursue persistently.

AFRICAN-AMERICAN PROVERB

Wise Things Your Grandma Told You

You are special.

Manners matter.

Treat others the way you want to be treated.

Your life can be what you want it to be.

Take the days one day at a time.

Always play fair.

Count your blessings, not your troubles.

Don't put limits on yourself.

It's never too late.

Put things back where you found them.

Decisions are too important to leave to chance.

Reach for the stars.

Clean up after yourself.

Nothing wastes more energy than worrying.

The longer you carry a problem, the heavier it gets.

Say "I'm sorry" when you've hurt someone.

A little love goes a long way.

Friendship is always a good investment.

Don't take things too seriously.

PATTI MACGREGOR
From *Family Times: Growing Together in Fun and Faith*

Nine Insights for Getting Ahead

1. Work hard

Follow tasks through to completion.

2. Think creatively

See challenges from new angles.

3. Speak gently

Consider the impact of your words.

4. Cooperate freely

Meet the need of the moment—even when it's not yours.

5. Act with integrity

Be the same privately as you are publicly.

6. Honor others

Recognize your coworkers' contributions.

7. See insightfully

Look beyond the obvious.

8. Listen thoroughly

Discern what is meant—not just what is said.

9. Respond appropriately

Deal with mistakes openly and fairly.

From *Insights for Living* newsletter

Extreme Virtues

1. Truth, if it becomes a weapon against persons.

2. Beauty, if it becomes vanity.

3. Love, if it becomes possessive.

4. Loyalty, if it becomes blind, careless trust.

5. Tolerance, if it becomes indifference.

6. Self-confidence, if it becomes arrogance.

7. Faith, if it becomes self-righteous.

ASHLEY COOPER
American columnist

Wisdom *for* Smart Living

Truth does not blush.

—TERTULLIAN

If one does not know to which harbor
he's headed, there is no such thing as a good wind.

—SENECA

My basic principle is that you don't
make decisions because they are easy;
you don't make them because they are cheap;
you don't make them because they are popular;
you make them because they're right.

—THEODORE HESBURGH

Do Good

Hate evil.

Cling to what is good.

Devote yourself to brotherly love.

Honor one another.

Be joyful.

Share with those in need.

Practice hospitality.

Rejoice with those who rejoice.

Mourn with those who mourn.

Avoid pride.

Do what is right.

Live at peace with one another.

Seek not revenge.

Do not be overcome by evil.

Overcome evil with good.

PAUL THE APOSTLE
Adapted from Romans 12:9–21

People Who Have It Together Have...

- *Self-awareness*

  These people know who they are. They know their abilities and strengths, what they are capable of doing, and how to accomplish it.

- *Confidence*

  They lack fear.

- *Self-worth*

  This is most often evidenced by their focus, not on themselves, but on those they serve and work with.

- *A sense of urgency*

  This means a "divine impatience" about everything they do.

- *A strong sense of personal mission*

  There is a vision of what needs to be done and a passion and focus about doing it.

- *Awareness and respect for their own uniqueness*

    They don't compare themselves to others or worry about what they're not. Their focus is on what they are.

- *A consistency to their lives*

    They are not tossed to and fro with every new idea or opportunity or change of events.

- *A sense of calmness and serenity*

    They are often people who can keep their heads when all about them are losing theirs.

HYRUM W. SMITH
Condensed from *What Matters Most: The Power of Living Your Values*

Ten Things That Really Matter

Always tell the truth.

Be sure you have all the facts before making a decision.

Keep open and friendly relations with God, family, and neighbors.

Devote time to helping others.

Review and adjust personal priorities on a regular basis.

Be financially responsible.

Discover "blind spots" by seeking advice from others.

Make hygiene a priority.

Become interdependent—we really do need each other.

Recognize God in daily life and explore the power of prayer.

DR. JOSEPH C. ALDRICH
President emeritus, Multnomah Bible College and Seminary

Words of Wisdom

- Nothing great was ever achieved without enthusiasm.

- All I have seen teaches me to trust the Creator for all I have not seen.

- Trust men and they will be true to you; treat them greatly and they will show themselves great.

- If we encountered a man of rare intellect, we should ask him what books he has read.

- Life is not so short but that there is always time enough for courtesy.

- Activity is contagious.

- Always do what you are afraid to do.

- The invariable mark of wisdom is to see the miraculous in the common.

- Our greatest glory consists not in never falling, but in rising up every time we fall.

- One of the most beautiful compensations of this life is that no one can sincerely try to help another without helping himself.

RALPH WALDO EMERSON
Poet and philosopher

Take Time

Take time to think;

  it is the source of your power.

Take time to play;

  it is the secret of your youth.

Take time to read;

  it is the foundation of your knowledge.

Take time to dream;

  it will take you to the stars.

Take time to laugh;

    it really is your best medicine.

Take time to pray;

    it is your touch with almighty God.

Take time to reach out to others;

    it will give your life significance.

GREGORY L. JANTZ, PH.D.
From *Becoming Strong Again*

A Final Prayer

Give me grace, good Lord…

To count the world as nothing,

To set my mind firmly on you,

To be content to be alone,

To depend on your comfort,

To suffer adversity patiently,

To be joyful for troubles,

To walk the narrow path that leads to life,

To keep the final hour in mind.

SIR THOMAS MORE
Sixteenth-century politician
Written just before he was beheaded

My List for Success

People I can contact for wisdom and perspective…

My List for Success

Books I want to read in the next year...

_____

_____

_____

_____

_____

_____

_____

_____

_____

_____

My List for Success

Habits I want to break…

My List for Success

Habits I want to form…

_____

_____

_____

_____

_____

_____

_____

_____

_____

_____

My List for Success

What I have learned from past failures…

_____

_____

_____

_____

_____

_____

_____

_____

_____

_____

_____

My List for Success

People I want to encourage…

_____

_____

_____

_____

_____

_____

_____

_____

_____

_____

My List for Success

Things I want to learn…

_____

_____

_____

_____

_____

_____

_____

_____

_____

_____

My List for Success

Goals for the next three years…

_____

_____

_____

_____

_____

_____

_____

_____

_____

_____

LISTS TO LIVE BY FOR EVERY MARRIED COUPLE

Offers tender, romantic, and wise ways to bring new life to marriage in a popular, easy-to-read format! This special collection of *Lists to Live By* is filled with gems of inspiration and timeless truths that married couples will treasure for a lifetime.

ISBN 1-57673-998-8

LISTS TO LIVE BY FOR EVERY CARING FAMILY

Provides inspiration on how to love, teach, understand, uplift, and communicate with children in topics such as "Helping Your Child Succeed," "Pray for Your Children," and "Four Ways to Encourage Your Kids." Parents will cherish each nugget of truth in this timeless special collection of *Lists to Live By*.

ISBN 1-57673-999-6

LISTS TO LIVE BY FOR SIMPLE LIVING

In our fast-paced, complex world, we all are looking for stillness, harmony, gentleness, and peace. The beauty of these eighty thoughtfully chosen lists is that they use simplicity to bring you simplicity—condensing essential information into one- or two-page lists.

ISBN 1-59052-058-0

LISTS TO LIVE BY FOR SMART LIVING

Reading a list is like having the best parts of a whole book gathered into a few words. Each list is a simple path to a better—smarter—life! If you read them, use them, and live them, you will become successful where it really matters—family, friendship, health, finance, business, wisdom, and faith.

ISBN 1-59052-057-2

Life-changing advice in a quick-to-read format!
LISTS TO LIVE BY

LISTS TO LIVE BY

This treasury of to-the-point inspiration—two hundred lists—is loaded with invaluable insights for wives, husbands, kids, teens, friends, and more. These wide-ranging ideas can change your life!
ISBN 1-57673-478-1

LISTS TO LIVE BY: THE SECOND COLLECTION

You'll get a lift in a hurry as you browse through this treasure trove of more *Lists to Live By*—with wisdom for home, health, love, life, faith, and successful living.
ISBN 1-57673-685-7

LISTS TO LIVE BY: THE THIRD COLLECTION

Two hundred lists with power, wisdom, inspiration, and practical advice. Some will make you reflect. Some will make you smile. Some will move you to action. And some will change your life.
ISBN 1-57673-882-5

THE STORIES FOR THE HEART SERIES

• More than 5 million sold in series!

• #1-selling Christian stories series!

Acknowledgments

Hundreds of books and magazines were researched, and dozens of professionals were interviewed for this collection. A diligent effort has been made to attribute original ownership of each list and, when necessary, obtain permission to reprint. If we have overlooked giving proper credit to anyone, please accept our apologies. If you will contact Multnomah Publishers, Inc., Post Office Box 1720, Sisters, Oregon 97759, with written documentation, corrections will be made prior to additional printings.

Notes and acknowledgments in this bibliography are shown in the order the lists appear, and in the styles designed by the sources. For permission to reprint the material, please request permission from the original source. The editors gratefully acknowledge the authors, publishers, and agents who granted permission for reprinting these lists.

Lists without attribution were complied by the editors.